S0-AZF-775

Johann Gutenberg

and the Amazing Printing Press

For Patricia

Copyright © 2003 by Bruce Koscielniak

Author acknowledges kind permission for use of Gutenberg Bible pages, and Jenson type
from *Johann Gutenberg: The Man and His Invention*, copyright © Albert Kapr, 1996;
English translation, copyright © Douglas Martin, 1996, Scolar Press, UK.

www.houghtonmifflinbooks.com

The text of this book is set in Adobe Caslon.
The illustrations are watercolor.

Library of Congress Cataloging-in-Publication Data

Koscielniak, Bruce.
Johann Gutenberg and the amazing printing press / Bruce Koscielniak.
p. cm.
Summary: A history of the modern printing industry, including how paper and ink are made,
looking particularly at the printing press invented by Gutenberg around 1450 but also at its precursors.
ISBN 0-618-26351-9
1. Printing—History—Origin and antecedents—Juvenile literature. 2. Books—History—
Juvenile literature. 3. Gutenberg, Johann, 1397?–1468—Juvenile literature. [1. Printing—
History. 2. Books—History. 3. Gutenberg, Johann, 1397?–1468.] I. Title.
Z126 .K58 2003
686.2—dc21
2002151176

Printed in Singapore
TWP 10 9 8 7 6 5 4 3 2 1

Johann Gutenberg
and the Amazing Printing Press

Bruce Koscielniak

HOUGHTON MIFFLIN COMPANY

BOSTON 2003

Books, books, books.
Soooo many books.
Ever wonder how it all got started—
all these books?

Printing! Someone, of course, has to write the book, but printing is the process that makes many copies of a book so that everyone who wants to can own or borrow one.

The story of the modern printing industry begins in Germany sometime around the year 1450, with a goldsmith named Johann Gutenberg (born about 1398, died 1468). His ideas for the design and use of a press to print efficiently from movable letter type brought about a practical revolution in the way books were produced and knowledge was spread.

The idea of printing—making multiple images mechanically—had been around long before Gutenberg. The Chinese are thought to have been the first printers. Having developed paper made of pulped mulberry bark, old fishnet, and rags in A.D. 105, and inventing lampblack (soot) inks a hundred years later, the Chinese were, by A.D. 868, skillfully block-printing sacred Buddhist texts on paper sheets that were pasted together into large rolls. Using a block of hard wood, they carved away the excess material, leaving only the raised characters, which would be inked for printing. Each Chinese character represents not a letter, but an idea. The Chinese language contains more than 30,000 characters, which made the printer's task difficult.

Paper is made by pouring bleached plant-fiber pulp onto a screen, pressing it flat, and allowing it to dry into a thin sheet.

Pine soot is collected, mixed with glue, and pressed into a mold to dry.

Woodblock

Inkstone

A stick of soot compound is mixed with water on the porous surface of an inkstone to make ink.

Roll book, or "scroll"

Before A.D. 1000, the Chinese were producing roll books made up of many sheets of paper—each sheet of the roll printed from a separate block. If part of a sheet needed to be changed, the entire block had to be carved again. Sometime around 1045, Pi Sheng, a Chinese printer, had the idea to use separate, coin-thin, fired-clay characters, which were pasted with tree resin and wax in rows on an iron plate, then inked, and paper was hand-rubbed on the printing plate. Using this method, the plate could be heated to soften the paste, and one or more characters on the plate could be changed. Pi Sheng was using movable type!

The next advance came in the 1200s when the Koreans, who had been employing Chinese woodblock printing methods since A.D. 700, decided to cast movable metal characters. They accomplished this task by making a character impression in clay and pouring a thin layer of molten bronze over it. The separate coinlike characters were fixed in a tray and inked to be printed by hand-rubbing paper on the type.

In Europe, beginning in about the year 1400, with a revival in learning under way and new demand for more books, experiments with printing from metal type were taking place in Italy and Holland. Europeans may have heard of metal type-making techniques in use in Korea, but they had to devise their own working methods independently.

By 1435, when Johann Gutenberg was living in Strasbourg (then a part of Germany) and beginning to work secretively on his new "tools" for printing letters of the alphabet, pen lettering was still the most efficient way to reproduce hundreds of readable words on a page. Except for some small block-printed picture books with few words, books in Europe at that time were copied by hand.

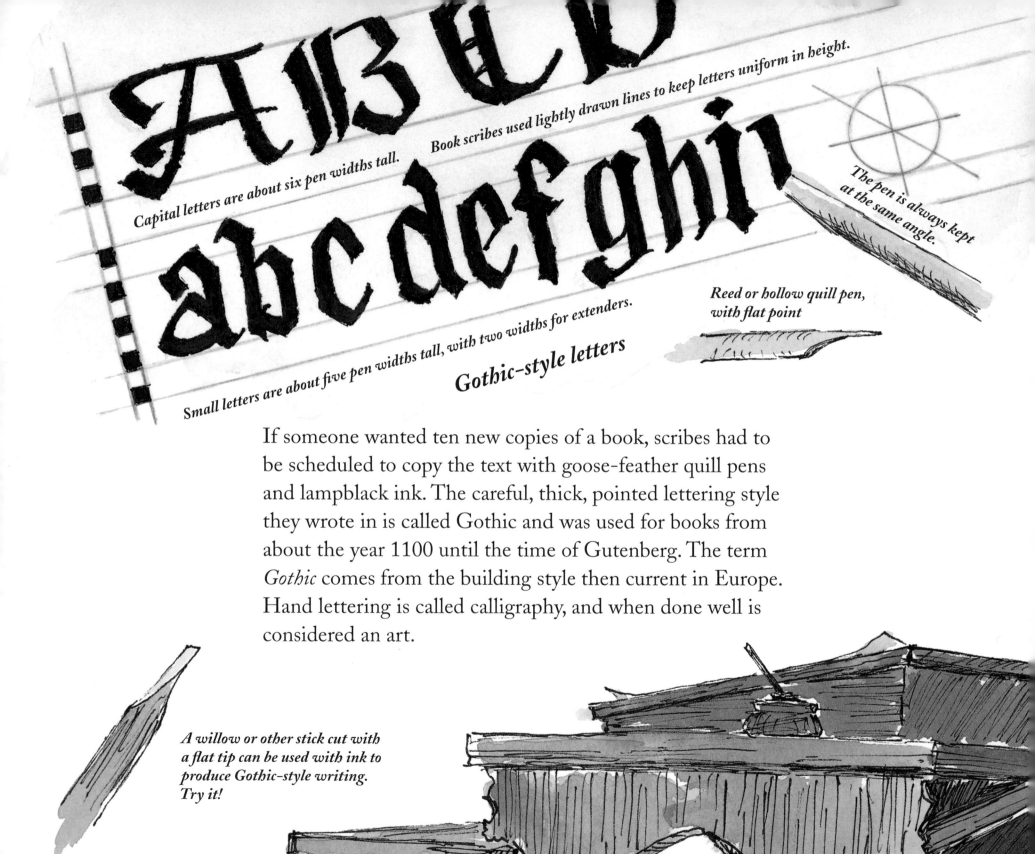

Capital letters are about six pen widths tall.

Book scribes used lightly drawn lines to keep letters uniform in height.

The pen is always kept at the same angle.

Small letters are about five pen widths tall, with two widths for extenders.

Reed or hollow quill pen, with flat point

Gothic-style letters

If someone wanted ten new copies of a book, scribes had to be scheduled to copy the text with goose-feather quill pens and lampblack ink. The careful, thick, pointed lettering style they wrote in is called Gothic and was used for books from about the year 1100 until the time of Gutenberg. The term *Gothic* comes from the building style then current in Europe. Hand lettering is called calligraphy, and when done well is considered an art.

A willow or other stick cut with a flat tip can be used with ink to produce Gothic-style writing. Try it!

Copy work was usually performed in monasteries, where scribes
lived and worked long days, tediously copying pages of text.
Fingers became numb from the work, and chilled hands had to
be warmed often during cold and damp winter months.

After the text was copied, each page would be embellished by artisans who specialized in painting headings called rubrics or rubrication, because of the ruby-red color used.

If a book was particularly important or a buyer wanted a highly decorated book, page ornaments and illustrations would be done with many painted colors and sheets of real gold beaten to the thickness of a moth's wing—called gold leaf. The art was so bright that it looked like light on the page and so was called illumination.

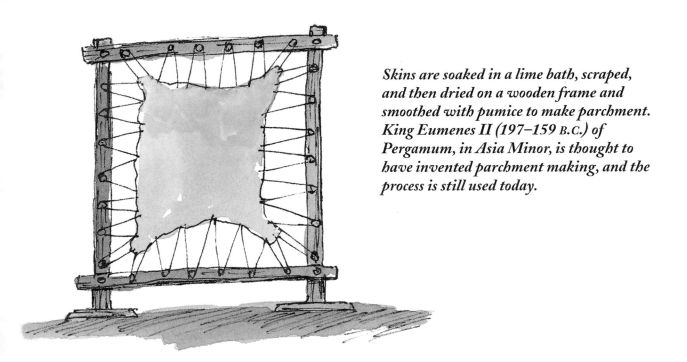

Skins are soaked in a lime bath, scraped, and then dried on a wooden frame and smoothed with pumice to make parchment. King Eumenes II (197–159 B.C.) of Pergamum, in Asia Minor, is thought to have invented parchment making, and the process is still used today.

Parchment, also known as vellum when it's of a very fine grade, was the material most commonly used for books during the Middle Ages in Europe. Made from the skin of goats, sheep, or lambs, parchment came into use in about 170 B.C. in the ancient world and continued in widespread use until after A.D. 1500. Its leather toughness and flexibility made this material well suited for book pages, which were expected to endure.

Papermaking finally came to Europe from China by way of the Silk Route across the Middle East in the year 1151, when paper was first made in Spain. Paper is more economical to produce and easier to work with than parchment, and gradually it replaced animal skins as writing material.

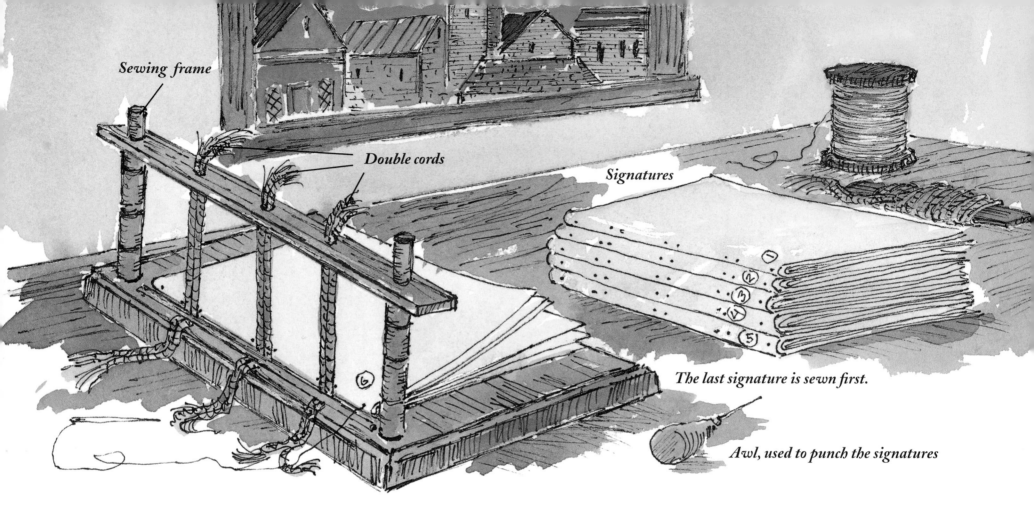

Sewing frame

Double cords

Signatures

The last signature is sewn first.

Awl, used to punch the signatures

Copied pages were assembled and fastened into a book in a process called binding. Instead of roll books, Europeans made books with folded pages, called codex books, which came into use in the Roman era. First, several sheets at a time were folded into numbered gatherings called signatures. Each signature was then sewn with thread along its folded edge, and it was also sewn onto heavy cords held perpendicular to the fold edge. A sewing frame was used to hold the signatures and cords in place.

Sewn headband

When all the signatures were firmly fastened to the cords, some additional reinforcement sewing was done. Thick, finished boards with smoothly beveled, or rounded, edges were attached to the cords at the front and the back of the book to form a rigid, protective cover. Leather was then wrapped around the book, glued to the boards, and decorated with "tooled" chiseled design work. All the material parts were made to work together beautifully, giving early books a feel of weight and substance.

Parchment was pasted down inside the board covers.

Leather straps with metal clasps to keep the book tightly closed

Oak or maple board

Tooling chisel

Double cords are fastened to the boards with wooden pegs.

Beveled edge

Vellum

Book covers were sometimes set with precious gemstones.

As each book required numerous artisans and many months to make, it's no surprise that books were not cheap! They were so valuable that only monasteries that had scribes in residence, libraries (which were open only to clergy and scholars), and some wealthy patrons could own books.

Ah, and everyone else? Well, most people didn't bother to learn to read because they had no access to books. Therefore, it was difficult for much of the population to learn about the world in which they lived.

The inventions of Johann Gutenberg are what made the printed word available and affordable to everyone—including you and me!

Gutenberg's important innovations were:

1. A new way to cast (form) pieces of movable metal type.
2. A new linseed-oil ink that would stick to metal type.
3. A press that would push the paper or vellum onto the inked type.

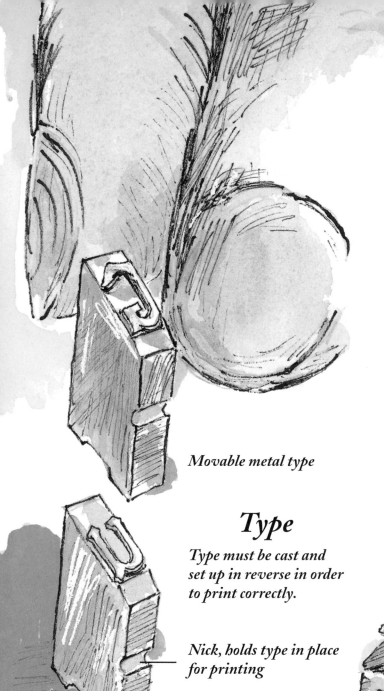

Movable metal type

Type

Type must be cast and set up in reverse in order to print correctly.

Nick, holds type in place for printing

Ink

Pressed from flaxseed, linseed oil is a thick, drying oil used in Gutenberg's time. It is still used today as a base for oil paint. Lampblack was added to the linseed oil to make printer's ink.

Ink daub, used to ink the type

Leather cover

Ink

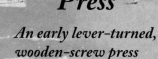

Press

An early lever-turned, wooden-screw press

Pouring Type

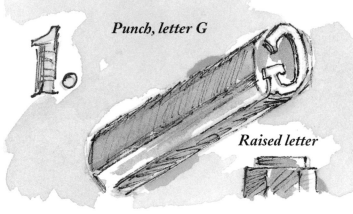

Punch, letter G

Raised letter

Gutenberg's printing type begins with a letter punch. Each letter and punctuation mark is cut in relief (with raised surface) and in reverse on a metal punch stick.

Metal matrix

A letter is punched into softer metal to make a matrix (letter mold).

Funnel

Type metals are melted.

The matrix is placed at the bottom of a box mold and filled with molten metal made of lead, tin, and antimony (a soft white metal). The mixture of metals, called an alloy, keeps type from shrinking or cracking.

The finished type is filed to smooth rough edges.

When the poured metal cools, the box mold is taken apart and the letter is cast in relief and in reverse.

A carpenter helped Gutenberg build a wooden printing press based on a cheese or wine press of the day. They may have used parts of an existing cheese or grape press.

Hundreds of pieces of metal type were stored in a case and "set" on a hand-held compositor's stick in reverse, that is, from right to left. The case contained more of the letters most frequently used, such as "A" and "E," and these compartments were positioned for easier access.

Type is transferred from the stick to a tray called a galley and inked to be checked for mistakes.

Copy page

Spacer bars

Form

When all the type to be printed on one side of a single sheet is ready, it is firmly fastened into a wood and metal frame called a form. A flat board would then be placed on the type and lightly tapped to level all the print surfaces.

By 1450, after many years of experimentation and refinements made to casting type and to perfecting inks and, of course, the printing press, Gutenberg had borrowed enough money to set up a print shop in his town of birth, Mainz, Germany, where the Main and Rhine Rivers meet.

Frisket, keeps paper clean

Tympanum, a thin cloth or leather surface on which the paper is placed

Type

The type in the form is inked, and dampened paper or vellum is placed on the tympanum and positioned on the type.

Printed pages are hung to dry.

A hand crank rolls the type form under the platen.

The platen, a heavy wood slab, is pushed down by the wooden screw and presses the paper onto the inked type to produce a good, clear imprint.

Printed books would now become available to meet the demand for books from schools, universities, churches, and people who simply wanted to read and learn new things.

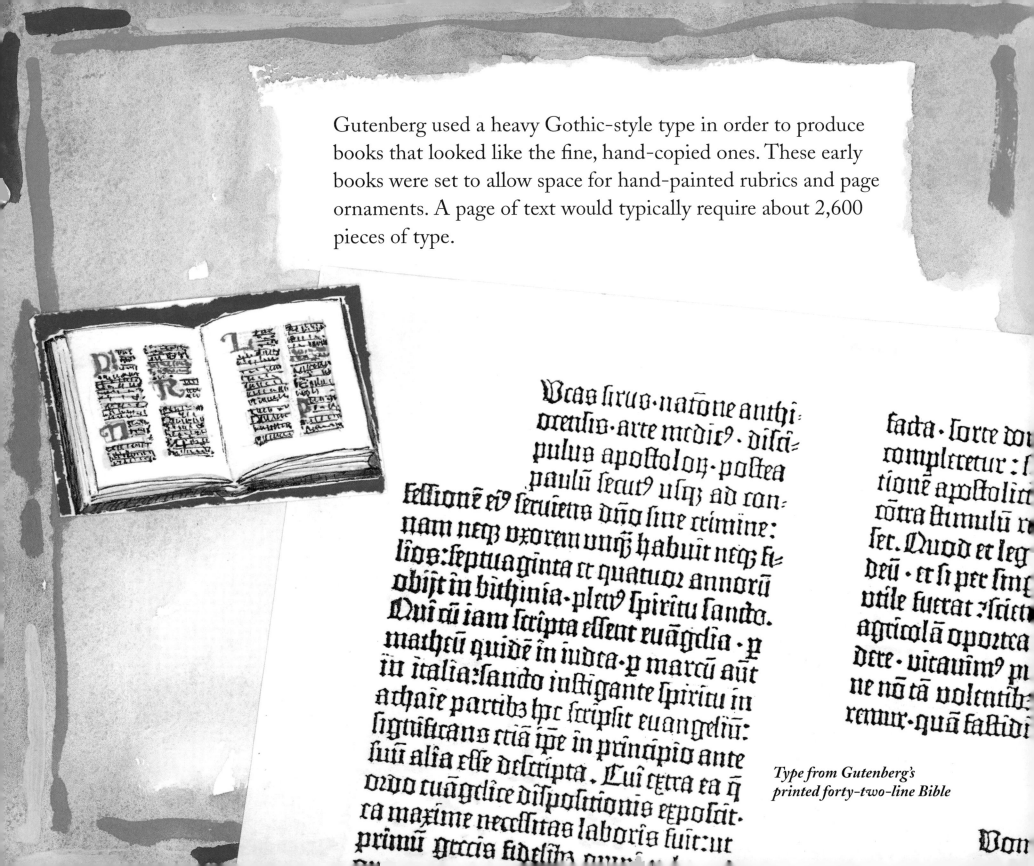

Gutenberg used a heavy Gothic-style type in order to produce books that looked like the fine, hand-copied ones. These early books were set to allow space for hand-painted rubrics and page ornaments. A page of text would typically require about 2,600 pieces of type.

Type from Gutenberg's printed forty-two-line Bible

Bookbinding was done by hand in the printer's workshop. Printed books were also commonly sold as loose sheets— leaving it to the buyer to hire someone to do rubrication, illumination, and binding of the buyer's choice.

Gutenberg never put his name or the date on his printed work, so it's not known for certain what his first books were—possibly he printed small grammar books, which were much in demand.

Unfortunately, in 1455, Johann Gutenberg lost his print shop
because he could not repay his loan on time.

Yet, it was also in 1455 that Gutenberg produced his most famous book—considered the first book printed from movable type in Europe—the majestic 1,282-page Latin Bible with two columns of forty-two lines of text per page. Today it is simply known as the Gutenberg Bible and is recognized as a monumental work of art. Gutenberg printed about two hundred copies of the Bible, and of those forty-seven copies exist today.

Gutenberg Bible

Jenson's type, printed in 1480

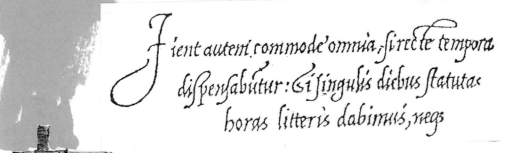

Printed "italic" type of the 1500s

Word of Gutenberg's achievement spread quickly, and people with interest in printing more books flocked to Mainz to see how this new art of the printing press was accomplished. Hundreds of print shops quickly opened, and soon thousands of different books were in print. Printers began to put their colophon, an identifying mark, on books they printed. Within a short time, easier-to-read type styles replaced the heavy Gothic type. Nicholas Jenson, in Venice, Italy, in the 1470s, designed a Roman alphabet that is still used today. In 1500, Aldus Manutius, also of Venice, created the well-known slanted *italic* type style.

We're looking for the printing shop...

Modern Roman-style type

Colophon, a printer's emblem

The amazing printing press had brought books to everyone. The rest, of course, is . . . well, we can read about it. And that's a good thing. Today we can read a book about anything from A to Z—and everything in between. Thanks, Mr. G.!